December 2003

To Mum + Dad,

Just a small gift to show you where I have settled with Andrea. I hope one day soon to show you around myself, so I hope this gives you a taste of what is to come. It is a fantastic city + well worth the trip!

All our love

Mark + Andrea

xxx

WELLINGTON
AND BEYOND

WELLINGTON
AND BEYOND

PHOTOGRAPHY BY
ROB SUISTED

KOWHAI

INTRODUCTION

Wellington is a city of intensity, challenge and diversity. Its weather can be extreme, its changes dramatic and definite. But while a northerly gale may buffet the city one day, a really bracing southerly the next, more often a rampaging storm will give way to uplifting, sun-drenched days when the air is still and the harbour sparkles like vintage champagne.

The city's topography is a challenge in itself. Homes perch precariously on steep hillsides rimming the harbour, and the downtown city stands almost entirely on reclaimed land. Wellingtonians rise to the physical challenge of their city with character and creativity. They are a diverse and cosmopolitan people. Sophisticated here, quirky there. In Wellington's lively cafés, restaurants, theatres and shops bureaucrats mix with *baristas*, diplomats with designers of fashion, performers with politicians, Maori with Mediterranean immigrants.

Geographically, Wellington is the centre of New Zealand and for hundreds of years has been the pivotal link in travel between the North and South Islands. Maori have lived around the region's harbours for about 700 years. European settlement began in 1839. Today greater Wellington, encompassing Porirua and Hutt Valley, is New Zealand's second largest urban area.

Since 1865, Wellington has been New Zealand's capital city, the nation's political and financial centre. But increasingly, the city is also referred to as the arts capital, cultural capital, festival capital and even café capital of New Zealand. Growing numbers of visitors come to the capital for its festivals (in particular the huge, biennial international arts festival), shows and sporting events. They come to tour Te Papa (Museum of New Zealand), art galleries, national archives and Parliament.

Sophisticated city the capital may be, but nature's heritage is also a very significant part of Wellington's special character. The harbour — Te Whanganui a Tara, or the Great Harbour of Tara — is considered one of the most picturesque in the world. In Maori tradition, the harbour holds special significance as the head of Te Ika a Maui, the great North Island

Looking across the entrance to Wellington Harbour with the Rimutaka Range in the distance.

fish caught by illustrious Polynesian ancestor Maui. Wellington's coastline sweeps from sandy beaches to surfing breaks to rocky outcrops — the domain of penguins, seals, dolphins and orca. Onshore, the city's suburbs merge with parks, reserves, wildlife sanctuaries and the expansive and cherished town belt.

Beyond Wellington city is New Zealand's 'centre stage'; showcasing the regions of Horowhenua, Wairarapa and Marlborough. These are productive, rural regions with farms, orchards, herb gardens and, within the last 20 years, internationally acclaimed wineries. In Marlborough and Wairarapa high sunshine hours, long, dry autumns and free-draining soils have been significant factors in the development of these regions' renowned wine industries.

This rich 'centre' of New Zealand also boasts outstanding natural heritage — on island wildlife sanctuaries, in forest parks and reserves, along the spectacularly rugged coastline of Wairarapa and throughout the myriad of forest-rimmed bays and inlets that make up the beautiful Marlborough Sounds.

Whether visitors to Wellington and the surrounding region come for a taste of city life, or to sample ecotourism, outdoor recreation, wine and food festivals, or even garden tours and country craft fairs, they will take away some very special memories.

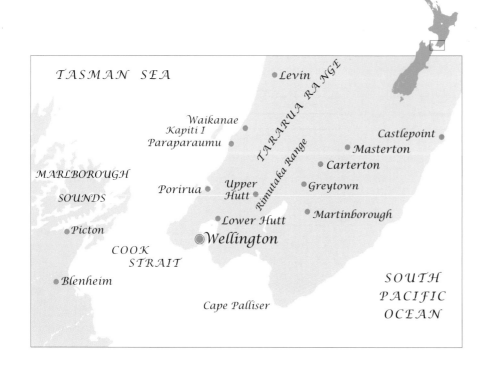

View of the city by night from Mt Victoria.

Oriental Bay's hillside villas (left), dominated by St Gerards Monastery on its landmark city site (above), rate among the most sought-after real estate in the capital. The Redemptionist Brothers built the Gothic-style monastery in 1932. In the foreground, pohutukawa flowers make their own design statement for nature.

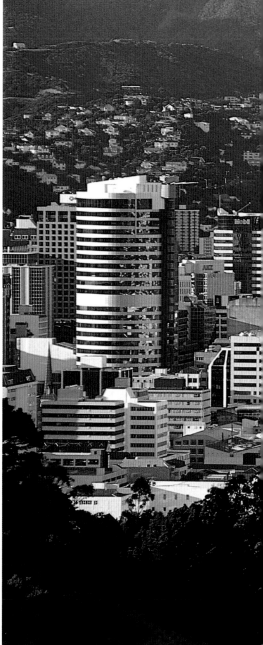

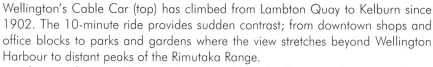

Wellington's Cable Car (top) has climbed from Lambton Quay to Kelburn since 1902. The 10-minute ride provides sudden contrast; from downtown shops and office blocks to parks and gardens where the view stretches beyond Wellington Harbour to distant peaks of the Rimutaka Range.

A feature of Victoria University 's campus (above) is the original Hunter Building, seen here on the centre left, which was built in 1906 and restored in the early 1990s.

Wellington's harbour edge originally lapped directly onto the surrounding forest-clad hills. Much of the central city, including the Wellington Sports Stadium (centre right) which was completed in 1999, has been built on reclaimed land.

Office towers are empty; the action's in the park. Concerts, outdoor theatre and cultural events bring people in their droves to Frank Kitts Park. The waterfront park, named after a longstanding city mayor, was developed in 1992.

Artist Sam Genet. Under the public eye, sculptors from around the world work their magic at the biennial Tareitanga Sculpture Symposium at Frank Kitts Park.

All New Zealanders who died in wars during the last 100 years are remembered here at the National War Memorial. The carillon tower, built in 1932, is one of the world's largest. The carillon's bells play daily.

Civic Square is a blend of cultures; interesting, vibrant and, at times, just a little different. Its designer, Ian Athfield, set tongues wagging with his striking steel and copper nikau palms.

The old Town Hall (top), a grand example of late Victorian municipal architecture, still plays a busy part in the city's cultural and administrative affairs.

'Cantilerper' (above) is a character in Wellington's annual Fringe Festival. And the people are unfazed!

On Wellington's City to Sea Bridge (top) a series of artworks incorporating whales, birds and fish symbolises the land meeting the sea. Artists are Paratene Matchitt and John Gray.

It seems ironic that the head office of New Zealand's Royal Forest and Bird Society (above) sits amid the noise and fumes of downtown Wellington. Artist Chris Finlayson's bright statement reflects the Society's raison d'être.

Wellington has a deserved reputation as 'café capital' of the world. And a reputation for colourful diversity!

Overleaf: Capital city — and another day of debate draws to a close. Like successive governments and their policies, the architectural styles of Parliament's buildings differ significantly. The granite and marble older building was completed in 1921; 'The Beehive' in 1970. (Inset): Question time in the legislative chamber.

Te Papa Tongarewa, the Museum of New Zealand, surpassed all expectations when it opened in 1998. Within the first seven months two million visitors had explored the museum's state-of-the-art displays. Through interactive computer technology, virtual reality, simulated film rides, live theatre and exhibitions, Te Papa brings to life New Zealand's stories, honours its achievements and displays its taonga (treasures). Te Papa also incorporates the award-winning Icon Restaurant, an espresso bar, café, and a range of conference facilities. The museum is open daily, and entry is free.

Bright colours, customwood and contemporary carvings that relate to all people of New Zealand, Maori and non-Maori, represent a dramatic and courageous break from tradition in Te Marae O Te Papa Tongarewa (left). This is a living marae operating within the museum.

Traditional carvings on the meeting house of Ngati Poneke, on Pipitea Marae, Thorndon Quay (above). People from the 'four winds' are welcome at this urban marae, built in the early 1980s on the historically significant harbourside site of Pipitea Pa.

Overleaf: Challenging performance by Nga Pauwai Maori Cultural Group at the annual Waitangi Day celebrations, Frank Kitts Park.

What better place to appreciate flowers and friends than the Wellington Botanic Garden (top, above and right) — a retreat for city dwellers and a treasure trove for garden lovers; a contrast of formal garden beds and rambling paths through remnant native forest. Features are the nationally acclaimed Lady Norwood Rose Garden, the tropical and temperate displays of the Begonia House, the 'Treehouse' education and environment centre, sculptures and stunning harbour views. Guided tours are available.

Surf's up at Lyall Bay — the city's popular surfing spot that's right beside the South Pacific's busiest airport. And the red-billed gulls wait for take-off.

Sandy beaches, rocky bays and surfing breaks — a gentle drive around Wellington's south coast will discover all of these, and none more than 10 minutes' drive from the city. Only the distant whitecaps give hint of the storms that sometimes savage this coast.

Choose your mode of transport. Sea kayaking (left) has recently become popular in Wellington Harbour.

Southern burst! After a southerly storm the air is crystalline, and across Cook Strait Tapu wae o Uenuku (2885 metres), the highest mountain of the Kaikoura range, seems close enough to touch.

Matiu, also known as Somes Island, the Wellington Harbour island that was for years inaccessible through its quarantine and internee camp uses, is now a nature reserve; a haven for rare tuatara — and open to the public.

Wellington and Hutt Valley cities (right) are hemmed by hills and harbour.

Wellington, or Venice? Remiro Bresolin's high-class, northern Italian Il Casino restaurant was the first of the exciting mix of cosmopolitan restaurants and cafés that now enrich downtown Wellington.

'Hey babe, do you have the time?' Quirky art on Marion Street.

The colourful selection at Monty Patel's Cuba Mall dairy epitomises the life of the mall itself, where the interesting, the alternative and the happy ethnic mix contribute significantly to the vibrancy of Wellington city. Cuba Mall has buskers and body-piercing studios, second-hand record and clothing stores, kebab stalls and cafés, funky bars and European bakeries.

'We're not sure what it's meant to be doing, but we love it anyway.' The infamous Cuba Mall bucket fountain.

Krazy Lounge Café, Cuba Mall. 'We only come here for the "krazy" patterns on the hot chocolate!'

Capital café culture; where there's a place for everyone, of all ages. Caffe L'Affare is also one of New Zealand's biggest wholesale coffee companies.

Waiting for the show at 'The Jimmy', the affectionate name for the magnificently restored St James Theatre. Theatre attendances in the 'arts capital' have exploded in recent years.

Per capita, there are more cafés in Wellington than New York City. It's little wonder the café culture thrives, when companies 'with attitude', such as Havana Coffee Works, supply the trade. Havana is true to the Cuban theme — the company is a major importer of Cuban green coffee beans and runs the zany Midnight Espresso café in Cuba Mall.

Early evening; and Courtenay Place gets ready to rock. Bars, restaurants and cafés; Middle East, Far East, French, Irish and universal themes; here is where it's at. A solid stout at Molly's for starters, perhaps?

Political puppets and satirical menus add intrigue to the Backbencher Pub, located appropriately just across the road from Parliament. Occasionally real politicians appear!

Character and contrast in Boulcott Street. Wellington's highest building dwarfs Bouquet Garni Restaurant — a French Renaissance villa which was once a doctor's surgery and then a bordello.

'At the going down of the sun, and in the morning, we will remember them . . .' Wellington Cenotaph.

Wellington Railway Station, built in 1937, was once New Zealand's largest public building.

Previous pages: Old Government Building, built in 1876 and restored in 1995, is the largest wooden building in the southern hemisphere. It once housed all the country's government departments.

Turnbull House was built in 1916 for Alexander Turnbull. His rare book collection is New Zealand's primary historic collection and his restored home is now a function centre.

Each year Wellington's Pacific Island peoples come together in a rousing celebration of their cultures at the Pacific Islands Festival in Frank Kitts Park. They bring with them song, dance and drums; colour, character and laughter. Here the Pacific Island Presbyterian Youth Group performs.

They may have left their tropical climes, but Wellington's 32 000-strong Pacific Island community adds a dimension of warmth and colour to the city. People from Samoa, Cook Islands, Tonga, Niue, Tokelau, Fiji and Tuvalu have lived in Wellington for several generations.

Roller blades or roses; anything goes on Wellington's harbour-side Oriental Parade.

Prow of the waka, or canoe, at Te Aro Park (above). Contemporary Maori art reflects earlier Maori occupation in the locality of this small, downtown spot, unofficially known as Pigeon Park.

The reincarnation of Blair Street — today, stylish restaurants, cafés and bars bring the trendy people to this colourful street. Fifty years ago, produce warehouses attracted delivery trucks. In the interim, a bold restoration programme by Blair Street proprietors and the city council has transformed the street and its grand warehouse facades.

Maori tradition relates how the taniwha (sea monster) Ngake gouged the entrance to Wellington Harbour. A second taniwha, Whataitai, was trapped by shallow water at low tide. Centuries later a great earthquake lifted Whataitai from the water and he died, becoming the present-day Hataitai Isthmus. Today ships, ferries and pleasure craft regularly ply the harbour entrance, and the peninsula beaches, in particular Scorching Bay (above), are favourite summer retreats for city folk. Across the harbour, the Eastbourne and Rimutaka hills are popular tramping areas.

A busy commercial harbour: interisland ferries run daily, cruise ships call during summer and the harbour's fishing fleet numbers over 30 boats (top). Wellington's port handles 4500 ship movements each year. Exports include meat, dairy and forestry products, imports are oil, consumer goods and cars.

Yachts at rest; sunset over Chaffers Marina (above). Wellington is not a 'city of sails' on the scale of its northern counterpart, Auckland, but yachting is neverthe-less a popular — and at times challenging — pastime.

The popularity of dragon boat racing — a long-time Asian passion — has recently exploded in Western countries. New Zealand is no exception. Corporate companies sponsor boats and crews representing business houses and schools compete with passion.

The annual dragon boat festival in Wellington Harbour attracts some 5000 paddlers and thousands of spectators pack vantage points around the city lagoon (left).

Yes! Sacred Heart College girls look justifiably pleased with their winning effort (top). Other crews look exhausted.

Is this what they call team building (above)? Rescue is on hand for a bailed-out corporate team.

Beach volleyball at Scorching Bay, Seatoun (top). And if exercise seems like too much trouble, lie back and watch the Cook Strait ferries cruising by, perhaps even spot a passing pod of dolphins or orca. It happens here!

For well over one hundred years, Wellington's delightful Basin Reserve cricket ground has been the focus for first-class matches (above). And not one parochial supporter in sight!

Participants in Sport Wellington's Round the Bays Fun Run and Walk pass Greta Point, near the start of the six-kilometre waterfront course (right).

Hurricanes! Hurricanes! The collective roar of several thousand rugby fans urges on their Super Twelve side (above). Be it a provincial game, a Super Twelve encounter or a test match, the Wellington crowd is always a passionate home team supporter — like most places in this rugby-crazed country.

The referee awards a scrum to the visiting team (right), and earns a slight frown from mascot Captain Hurricane (above right) for his decision.

No other playground has a slide like this! The lighthouse slide, topped with seagull wind vane, beckons the young in Frank Kitts Park. Little wonder the park won landscape design awards when first developed.

Previous pages: Wellington's magnificent English Gothic-style Old St Pauls Cathedral. Built in 1866, using totara, matai, kauri and rimu, it was was gifted to the people in 1966. Entry is by donation.

It must be Sunday. Only the rowers ruffle the calm waters, as the city's two tallest buildings stand sentinel over early morning downtown Wellington. As the city wakes, the harbour will ripple with kayaks, yachts and fizz boats; the waterfront will buzz with runners, roller bladers and icecream-eating families, cafés will churn out countless long blacks and frothy cappuccinos. Then will come Monday, and the office towers will hum with life once more.

Avant-garde at the races. Local fashion designers — and personalities — enjoy their time in the spotlight as the innovative finalists are announced for the Wellington Cup 'Fashion in the Field' awards, 1999. Did she really drink all that champagne?

Bats Theatre is considered the 'nest' of Wellington's thriving theatre scene. Many young actors have started their careers here, while established performers such as Miranda Harcourt (left) and Dame Kate Harcourt (on the steps) still support the friendly venue.

'I think I'd rather be in this jungle.' Or perhaps, '. . . one day it will all be mine.' Just what is this chimpanzee contemplating, as he overlooks the city's office towers from his own high-rise spot at the Wellington Zoo? The zoo's chimp colony is the second largest in Australasia and part of an international chimpanzee breeding programme.

'Wow Mum! How did that otter move so fast!' Youthful delight at Wellington Zoo.

International zoos are moving away from a cage mentality and developing more natural habitats for the animals in their care. Wellington Zoo is no exception. There is not a bar or wire in sight in the zoo's Tropical River Trail, where several species of primates swing through rain forest and pelicans glide from island to island, in one of New Zealand's largest wildlife habitat exhibits.

Orca are regular harbour visitors.

The first Petone wharf (above) was built in 1883 for meat transportation by the Gear Meat Company.

Because of simultaneous road and rail development the current wharf, built in 1909, has had little use — although locals today enjoy the fishing and swimming opportunities.

Previous pages: Wellington City and Te Whanganui a Tara, the Great Harbour of Tara. Tara was one of the first people to enter the harbour after the legendary Maori explorer Kupe who visited here in around 950AD. Today's view from Mt Kaukau must be vastly different from the one seen by those early travellers.

During the week commuters ride ferries from Days Bay wharf on the eastern side of the harbour to the city. In the weekends, city folk cross to the cafés, beaches and bush walks of the eastern bays.

It's a big party day for Wellington, when over 20 000 people flock to Trentham Race-course for the third-richest thoroughbred race in New Zealand, the Wellington Cup. Trentham, which has been a racing club since 1906, holds 15 other race meetings during the year and is also a popular venue for conferences and weddings.

The Clerk of the Course is seen here in the birdcage (left), while happy jockey Leanne Isherwood leads the field on Wellington Cup winner, Miss Bailey (top).

Can we trust these scales? After the race, this jockey (above) comes eye to eye with the Clerk of the Scales.

What to do on a Wellington weekend? Perhaps take a ride on Bob the Clydesdale at Staglands Wildlife Reserve in the Akatarawa Valley, Upper Hutt, north of Wellington city. Or a picnic, at this popular spot where city folk meet the country.

Local enthusiasts call Wellington the mountain bike capital of the world! With a huge network of recreational riding tracks and one dedicated mountain bike park, the claim is not outrageous. Several national racing events are held in the region, such as the Mt Climie Downhill and famous Karapoti Classic.

Thirty minutes' drive north of Wellington is the modern, multi-cultural city of Porirua. The name means 'Two Harbours' — and while there is much scope for swimming in the sea, if the day is hot then any water will do: like this ornamental pond at the city's Aotea Lagoon.

Previous pages: Kapiti Island, just northwest of Wellington, is one of New Zealand's largest and most significant island sanctuaries; a safe haven for many endangered wildlife species. This stunning view is from Colonial Knob Scenic Reserve.

Porirua market — a weekly phenomenon that's exploded from small beginnings as a Lions Club fundraiser. Officially it starts at 6am, but from midnight on, stall holders in this satellite city, 21 kilometres north of the capital, are setting up their produce, second-hand goods and hot food stalls. Like the people of Porirua who flock to the market, the food comes from all cultures.

Home time for the thousands of commuters who escape the city bustle each day and travel by car or train to coastal towns north of Wellington. The first outlier is Plimmerton (above), named after prominent early Wellington businessman, John Plimmer.

Is this relationship bonding or what? Tandem parapenting over Paekakariki Hill, just over 40 kilometres north of Wellington. In the distance, the South Island beckons.

The dauntingly rugged western cliffs of Kapiti Island on its ocean side, as spied from a venture-some glider. The Kapiti coast, 52 kilometres northeast of Wellington, is a spectacularly scenic region to experience 'the freedom of flight', promised by the Paraparaumu-based Wellington Gliding Club.

'We live here for the sunsets.' This oft-heard comment from Plimmerton residents rings true, as the sinking sun plays colourful havoc with clouds over Mana Island. The island, which lies 7 kilometres west offshore from the entrance to Porirua Harbour, is a noted wildlife sanctuary, home to several threatened species including takahe and little spotted kiwi.

Wet and wild. From Porirua's Whitireia Park one can watch the ups and downs of windsurfing at Plimmerton Beach.

Ridgelines from Karori to Kaikoura. The view is from Colonial Knob Scenic Reserve (just 20 minutes' drive from downtown Wellington) looking south across the Karori hills to the South Island's Kaikoura Mountains.

Mana marina has a strategic location by the entrance to Porirua Harbour and Pauatahanui Inlet, near fishing grounds and Cook Strait. This area (also known as Paremata Point) is the oldest area of continuous occupation in the Wellington region.

Paekakariki and Paraparaumu townships, from Paekakariki Hill. Little wonder many city workers choose to live 'up the coast'. The trials of daily commuting are easily assuaged when weekends and long summer evenings promise relaxing hours of beach walks, swimming and fishing, or perhaps just watching sunsets.

Intricate patterns at the Raumati Beach sand sculpture competition, north of Wellington.

Black sands and black suits — Kapiti Women's Triathlon competitors head for the sea.

A little further north nature's hand is played in more gentle form, as shown by this flourishing field at the Te Horo Stone Pine Creek lavender farm, approximately 70 kilometres north of Wellington. The lavender is harvested by hand then distilled with rainwater to produce essential oil, renowned for its therapeutic qualities.

Browsing in the buttercups — Jersey heifers in Horowhenua. This rural region, north of Wellington, is an important source of produce for the city. Orchards and herb gardens, market gardens and dairy farms fill the fertile plains.

Coastal dunes, Lake Horowhenua, the towering Tararua Ranges — and nestled in between, the township of Levin, principal service centre for the rural industries of the surrounding Horowhenua Plains. Levin is also known for its racecourse, motor racing circuit, popular beaches (just a few kilometres west of the town) and handy access eastwards into the tramping tracks of Tararua Forest Park.

The Tararua Ranges, extending from the head of the Hutt Valley, about 48 kilometres northeast of Wellington, dominate the southern North Island skyline, and for years have lured adventurous folk to their windswept peaks and tussocked ridgelines, deep gorges and forest-covered river flats. Tararua, now managed by the Department of Conservation, was the first of 19 forest parks created in New Zealand for their conservation and recreation values. Tramping and deerstalking are traditional Tararua pastimes.

Ever alert red deer — hind and yearling on the bush edge.

Deerstalkers cross the Waingawa River.

Overleaf: Mass ascension. Balloons in the International Hot Air Balloon Fiesta fill the Carterton sky, about 92 kilometres northeast of Wellington, with a simultaneous lift off. And yes, that is Thomas the Tank Engine — 65 feet long and not a railway line in sight!

Dragon boat racing has become extremely popular throughout New Zealand. Lake Henley, Masterton, is the venue for the annual Wairarapa Regional Championships. Masterton, just over 100 kilometres north of Wellington, is the Wairarapa's largest centre.

Greytown, in the southern Wairarapa, boasts New Zealand's 'most complete' main street of wooden Victorian architecture. Buildings such as Kouka Cottage, built in 1868 and now a glassworks studio, have been lovingly restored and resurrected as craft galleries, cafés and antique shops.

This Pukeko wind toy comes from Moazark, a delightfully innovative and patriotic Martinborough whirligig manufacturer.

Roses and restorations. The southern Wairarapa town of Martinborough, 84 kilometres northeast of Wellington, was first established as a farming centre, but in recent years has undergone a transformation along with the meteoric development of the region's wine industry.

As well as vineyard patrons who regularly visit the town, thousands of visitors gather each year for Toast Martinborough, a nationally renowned wine, food and music festival, and for the biannual Martinborough Fair, a massive country fair set around the town's distinctive square (left).

A landmark building among the town's shops, cafés and wineries is the Martinborough Hotel (above). Built in 1888, and recently restored to such a standard as to be listed among the world's leading boutique hotels, the hotel's restaurant often features local winemakers' dinners.

Tasting at Ata Rangi Vineyard. Free-draining soils and low autumn rainfall help make Martinborough an internationally acclaimed wine region. A high proportion of red wine grape plantings and a particular reputation for pinot noir distinguishes Martinborough from other wine areas.

Jam session in January. While the annual Toast Martinborough festival has become something of a phenomenon, traditionally sold out within hours of tickets
going on sale, other, smaller events, like the Te Kairanga Vineyard music festival,
draw wine lovers, families and friends to savour the special, laid-back Martinborough
atmosphere.

Overleaf: Castlepoint (Rangiwhakaoma); one
of the most spectacular spots on the Wairarapa
coast, a little over an hour's drive from Masterton. The sheltered lagoon, fossil-rich limestone
reef, sand dunes and Castle Rock itself are all
part of Castlepoint Scenic Reserve. There are
several walking tracks in the vicinity.

The small Cape Palliser fishing settlement of Ngawi is squeezed on a narrow coastal strip in southern Wairarapa between salt-laden, windswept hills and the southern ocean.

No boat is required for these surfcasting hopefuls fishing on the sandspit beside Lake Onoke outlet. Onoke, also known as Lake Ferry, is a popular fishing and bird watching spot with the added attractions of a seaside hotel and camping ground.

As the South Pacific Ocean surges into Palliser Bay, the Cape Palliser lighthouse on the most southerly tip of the North Island signals its warning to coastal shipping. This is a bleak yet beautiful piece of coastline to visit; the Cape Palliser road wends its narrow way beneath steep coastal bluffs on one side and surging surf and rocky outcrops on the other. Along the way are the quaint settlements of Te Kopi and Ngawi, walking detours into Haurangi Forest Park and the stunning Pinnacle limestone formations, surfcasting beaches and shellfish spots, the largest fur seal breeding colony in the North Island and, finally, the lighthouse. Only 250 steps to climb!

In today's world, where urban sprawl has encroached so much on natural habitats, it is a pleasure to see so many examples of native wildlife living in or close to Wellington city.

New Zealand fur seal colonies (left) are easily accessible at Red Rocks, on Wellington's south coast, and in Palliser Bay.

Common gecko (top) live throughout the Wellington region.

Little blue penguins (above) have been known to 'move in' uninvited beneath coastal houses and garages in the region.

Unlike the southern, glacial gouged fiords, the Marlborough Sounds — in the northeast of the South Island — are drowned river valleys; a boatie's paradise of inlets, channels and sheltered bays. Early settlers tried to link these remote bays by land, but their bridle paths are now used only by trampers. In the Sounds, water is the way to travel.

A bird's eye view across the northern tip of the Sounds towards Arapawa Island and, in the distance, Wellington (top).

From capital city to the calm of the Sounds. The Cook Strait ferry services (above) are a vital link between the North and South Islands.

Morning reflection. Yachts in Waikawa Bay marina (right), in the western reaches of the Sounds, await their next cruise.

Welcome to the South Island. Peace and calm on the immaculately groomed Picton foreshore can be a welcome contrast for interisland ferry passengers just arrived from Wellington city.

Previous pages: Hues of blues. Last view of the day, looking westwards over Pelorus Sound from Mt Stokes (1203 metres), the highest point of the Marlborough Sounds.

Colourful patterns in colourful Blenheim, which began as a service town in the Marlborough region for pastoral and cropping farmers (with an 1860s gold rush thrown in) and now also serves growing wine and tourism industries. Blenheim Railway Station (built early 1900s) is the town's travel centre.

In the last 25 years the New Zealand wine industry has burgeoned. Leading the way has been Marlborough which, through a unique combination of special soil conditions and climate, has become a premier grape-growing region.

Allan Scott Winery, a family owned vineyard, winery and restaurant (top).

Have they finished tasting yet? Ian Lyall's horse and cart transport (above); a delightful way to meander from winery to winery.

Artist in residence at Hunters Winery, Clarry Neame (right). Hunters is a pioneer Marlborough winery which regularly wins international awards and accolades.

A scenic lunch stop for wildlife spotters. Ecotourists on Les and Zoe Battersby's Dolphin Watch Marlborough excursion call at Motuara Island Bird Sanctuary, a wonderful, predator-free Department of Conservation reserve in the Marlborough Sounds.

Hot, dry summers are the norm in Marlborough. Climate is a major factor for the transformation of the region from one dominated by pastoral farming into New Zealand's major grape-growing area. Will the Waiohopai Valley be the next to change?

Overleaf: The full moon takes centre stage over Wellington and beyond. What will tomorrow bring? View from Mt Stokes, Marlborough Sounds, looking over Cape Jackson.

First published in 1999 by New Holland Kowhai
an imprint of New Holland Publishers (NZ) Ltd
Auckland • Sydney • London • Cape Town

218 Lake Road, Northcote, Auckland, New Zealand
14 Aquatic Drive, Frenchs Forest, NSW 2086, Australia
86-88 Edgware Road, London W2 2EA, United Kingdom
80 McKenzie Street, Cape Town 8001, South Africa

ISBN: 1-877246-24-7

Managing editor: Renée Lang
Design: Chris O'Brien

3 5 7 9 10 8 6 4 2

Colour reproduction by Colour Symphony Pte Ltd
Printed by Times Offset (M) Sdn Bhd